Gems & Imagen 3

Google's AI Game-Changer - Review and Everything You Should Know

Exploring the Gemini Upgrade and the Innovations Set to Transform Our Everyday Lives

Alejandro S. Diego

1

Table of Contents

Introduction

In recent years, artificial intelligence has advanced at an unprecedented pace, transforming various facets of technology and everyday life. Google has been at the forefront of this evolution, consistently pushing the boundaries of what AI can achieve. The Gemini AI platform stands as one of the most significant milestones in this journey. With the introduction of "Gems" assistants and the Imagen 3 image generation model, Google has unveiled tools that could reshape our understanding and use of artificial intelligence.

The Gemini AI platform isn't just another step forward in AI development; it's a leap. "Gems" are personalized AI assistants designed to cater to individual needs, offering a level of specialization that general-purpose AI models cannot match. Whether it's aiding in complex coding tasks, providing marketing insights, or managing day-to-day activities, Gems represent a new era of customized digital assistance. This level of personalization marks a shift in how AI is perceived and utilized, moving from a one-size-fits-all approach to a more nuanced and user-centric experience.

Then there's Imagen 3, which takes AI-generated imagery to a new level. In a world where visual content is king, the ability to generate high-quality, photorealistic images from simple text prompts is nothing short of revolutionary. Imagen 3 doesn't just create images; it crafts art. This capability opens up new possibilities for industries such as advertising, digital art, and virtual reality, where the demand for striking visuals is ever-growing. By blending reality and imagination, Imagen 3 sets a new standard for AI's role in creative processes.

The implications of these advancements are far-reaching. We're not just talking about incremental improvements to existing technologies; we're looking at a fundamental change in how AI integrates with our daily lives. From enhancing productivity and creativity to making complex tasks more accessible, Gemini's upgrades have the potential to touch every aspect of our world. These tools are not limited to tech enthusiasts or large corporations; they are designed to be accessible to everyone, democratizing the power of AI in ways previously thought impossible.

But why focus on these developments now? The field of AI is evolving rapidly, and understanding these changes is crucial. With new tools and platforms emerging almost daily, it can be challenging to keep up with the pace of innovation. This book aims to bridge that gap by providing an in-depth analysis of Google's latest contributions to the AI landscape. It seeks to break down the complexities of the Gemini platform, making it understandable and relevant to a broad audience. By exploring these advancements in detail, the book hopes to offer insights into the future of AI and its potential to transform various aspects of our lives.

In a world increasingly shaped by artificial intelligence, knowledge is power. Understanding the capabilities and limitations of these new tools allows us to harness their potential effectively and responsibly. This book serves as a guide through the intricacies of Google's Gemini platform, offering a comprehensive look at what makes these advancements unique and why they matter. As we stand on the cusp of a new era in AI development, there's no better time to explore the transformative power of tools like Gems and Imagen 3.

Chapter 1: The Genesis of Gemini

Google's journey in the field of artificial intelligence has been a story of consistent innovation and bold strides. From its early days of improving search algorithms to becoming a key player in AI research and development, Google has always aimed to push the boundaries of what technology can achieve. The company's evolution in AI began with integrating machine learning into its core products, like Google Search and Google Maps, to provide users with more accurate and personalized results. Over time, this laid the groundwork for more complex and ambitious projects, leading to the creation of tools and platforms that leverage AI in groundbreaking ways.

One of the earliest and most notable milestones in Google's AI history was the development of TensorFlow, an open-source machine learning framework that quickly became a staple in AI research and application. This platform allowed developers and researchers to build and train neural networks more efficiently, democratizing access to powerful AI tools. TensorFlow's release marked a turning point, not just for Google, but for the broader AI community, as it paved the way for more sophisticated models and applications.

Building on the success of TensorFlow, Google continued to expand its AI capabilities through various projects and acquisitions. The company invested heavily in natural language processing, resulting in the creation of models like BERT (Bidirectional Encoder Representations from Transformers), which significantly improved the way machines understand and generate human language. These advancements made their way into products like Google Assistant, offering users a more intuitive and conversational experience.

Another major leap in Google's AI evolution came with the development of DeepMind, an AI research lab acquired by Google in 2015. DeepMind's work, particularly in reinforcement learning, led to groundbreaking achievements like AlphaGo, the first AI to defeat a world champion Go player. These successes showcased the potential of AI to tackle complex, strategic tasks that were once thought to be beyond the reach of machines.

All these developments set the stage for the Gemini platform, which represents a strategic culmination of Google's AI endeavors. Unlike previous efforts that focused on specific areas like language processing or reinforcement learning, Gemini aims to bring a more holistic approach to AI. The platform integrates various aspects of artificial intelligence, including machine learning, natural language processing, and computer vision, to create a suite of tools that are not only powerful but also versatile.

The strategic vision behind Gemini is to make AI more accessible and tailored to individual needs. This is where "Gems" come into play, offering specialized AI assistants that can be customized to perform specific tasks exceptionally well. Google recognizes that the future of AI lies not in creating general-purpose models that try to do everything, but in developing specialized tools that can deliver precise and meaningful results. This shift towards specialization reflects a deeper understanding of how AI can be most effectively utilized in different contexts.

In addition to the Gems, Gemini introduces Imagen 3, an advanced image generation model that blurs the line between reality and imagination. This move indicates Google's commitment to expanding AI's role in creative fields, providing tools that empower users to produce high-quality, photorealistic images with ease. The combination of Gems and Imagen 3 showcases Google's strategic intent to cover a broad spectrum of AI applications, from task-specific assistants to creative tools.

The launch of Gemini marks a pivotal moment in Google's AI evolution, embodying the company's vision of making advanced artificial intelligence accessible to a wider audience. By focusing on both the practicality and creativity of AI, Google aims to provide tools that can transform not just industries but everyday experiences. The Gemini platform stands as a testament to Google's belief in the transformative power of AI and its potential to redefine the way we interact with technology in the years to come.

The introduction of "Gems" within the Gemini platform represents a new chapter in the evolution of artificial intelligence. Unlike traditional AI models that often take a generalized approach, Gems are designed to be hyperspecialized, focusing on specific tasks to offer a more tailored and effective experience. This specialization allows users to create personal experts in various fields, whether it's coding, marketing strategies, or managing everyday tasks. The rollout of Gems signals a shift in AI from broad, catch-all solutions to highly individualized assistants that cater to specific needs.

What sets Gems apart is their ability to be customized, acting almost like a bespoke service tailored to each user's requirements. Instead of trying to be a jack-of-all-trades, these assistants excel in their designated areas, providing users with a depth of expertise that general-purpose AI models can't match. For instance, a Gem created for coding assistance won't just provide generic programming advice; it can be trained to understand the intricacies of the user's specific project, offering insights and solutions that are directly relevant. This level of specialization ensures that users get more accurate, relevant, and actionable responses, enhancing productivity and decision-making.

Traditional AI assistants, such as general-purpose chatbots or virtual assistants like Siri and Alexa, are designed to handle a wide array of tasks. They answer questions, set reminders, play music, and provide weather updates, but they often lack the depth required for more complex or niche tasks. They function as helpful aides but are limited by their generalized programming. Gems, on the other hand, are built with a different philosophy. By honing in on a particular domain, they provide an experience akin to having a personal expert or consultant, bringing a level of depth and precision that generalized models can't offer.

The rollout of Gems is also noteworthy for its inclusivity. Google is making these specialized AI assistants accessible to a wide range of users, from small businesses to freelancers and students. This democratization of AI technology is a crucial aspect of the Gemini platform's strategic vision. It's not just about providing powerful tools to large enterprises with big budgets; it's about making these advanced capabilities available to anyone, anywhere. By doing so, Google aims to level the playing field, allowing individuals and small organizations to harness the power of AI to elevate their capabilities and compete on a larger scale.

Moreover, Gems are not static; they can be continually refined and improved over time. Users can provide feedback and input that allow these assistants to learn and adapt, becoming even more effective at their designated tasks. This dynamic nature means that the more a Gem is used, the better it becomes at serving its specific function. This adaptability is key in a world where the pace of change is accelerating, and the ability to quickly learn and evolve is a valuable asset.

The launch of Gems signifies a bold move towards creating AI that is not just functional but transformational. By focusing on task-specific expertise, these assistants offer a glimpse into the future of AI, where the emphasis is on delivering precise, meaningful, and context-aware assistance. This approach not only enhances user experience but also sets a new standard for what AI can achieve. In a market crowded with general-purpose models, Gems stand out by offering a level of customization and specialization that promises to change the way we think about and use artificial intelligence in our daily lives.

Chapter 2: Gems – Personalized AI Assistants

Gems are a revolutionary concept in the world of artificial intelligence, representing a new breed of specialized AI assistants designed to cater to specific needs with exceptional precision and expertise. Unlike the broad and often generic capabilities of traditional AI models, Gems are purpose-built to focus on particular tasks or areas of knowledge, functioning almost like personal experts that can be tailored to individual users. This level of specialization allows them to deliver highly relevant and effective assistance, transforming the way users interact with AI.

At their core, Gems are designed to bridge the gap between general AI and the demand for more nuanced, task-specific solutions. While general-purpose AI, such as popular virtual assistants, can perform a wide range of functions—like setting reminders, answering basic queries, or providing weather updates—they often lack the depth required for more complex or specialized tasks. Gems, however, are built to excel in specific domains. Whether it's coding, marketing strategy, data analysis, or even creative tasks like content generation, Gems are tailored to understand and address the intricacies of these areas with a level of detail and accuracy that general models simply can't match.

The concept behind Gems revolves around creating personal experts that adapt to the unique requirements of each user. For instance, a marketing professional can use a Gem specifically designed to analyze market trends, identify target demographics, and suggest effective strategies, acting almost like a virtual marketing consultant. Similarly, a student struggling with advanced mathematics could have a Gem tutor that not only provides explanations but also identifies their learning gaps and offers personalized exercises to enhance understanding. This level of customization means that Gems are not just tools; they become partners in the user's journey, providing support that is directly aligned with individual goals and challenges.

What makes Gems particularly groundbreaking is their adaptability. Users can customize these assistants to suit their specific needs, providing input that allows the AI to learn and refine its responses over time. This iterative process means that a Gem doesn't just start as a generic expert; it becomes increasingly attuned to the user's preferences and requirements, offering progressively more refined and valuable assistance. The ability to personalize and evolve with the user is a defining characteristic of Gems, setting them apart from static AI models that offer limited flexibility.

Furthermore, the creation of Gems is not limited to a select few; it's a democratized process that enables a broad range of users to benefit from advanced AI expertise. Whether you're a freelancer looking for an edge in your work, a small business owner trying to streamline operations, or an individual seeking to enhance personal productivity, there's the potential to create a Gem that fits your specific needs. This approach empowers users to harness the full potential of AI, regardless of their technical background or resources, making specialized AI assistance accessible to all.

In summary, Gems represent a paradigm shift in artificial intelligence by offering specialized, customizable assistance that transforms the AI-user relationship. They move beyond the limitations of general-purpose models to provide a level of expertise and adaptability that can make a tangible difference in various fields. By allowing users to create personal experts tailored to their unique needs, Gems redefine what it means to interact with AI, turning it into a more meaningful and impactful experience. This innovation opens up new possibilities for how AI can be integrated into daily life, making it an indispensable tool for personal and professional growth.

The concept of democratizing AI has been a driving force behind the development and rollout of Gems within Google's Gemini platform. Traditionally, the most advanced and powerful AI tools have been accessible primarily to large enterprises with significant resources, leaving smaller businesses, independent professionals, and the general public at a disadvantage. Gems seek to change this dynamic by making specialized, high-level AI assistance available to a much broader audience, effectively leveling the playing field in an increasingly digital world.

Gems bring advanced AI capabilities directly to individuals, small businesses, and organizations that might not have the resources to develop or deploy such technology on their own. By offering these specialized assistants in a user-friendly and accessible manner, Google ensures that everyone, regardless of their technical expertise or budget, can benefit from the power of AI. This move marks a significant step toward inclusivity in the tech world, where the benefits of AI are no longer confined to those with the means to invest heavily in custom solutions.

One of the key aspects of democratizing AI through Gems is their adaptability and ease of customization. Unlike traditional AI systems that often require a deep understanding of machine learning and complex programming, Gems can be tailored by the user to meet specific needs with minimal technical input. This means that a small business owner can create a Gem to handle tasks like customer service, data analysis, or marketing strategy without needing a team of AI specialists. Similarly, a freelancer can develop a Gem to assist with project management or client communication, gaining an edge in their field without incurring the costs typically associated with high-end AI tools.

Moreover, the global availability of Gems across over 150 countries underscores Google's commitment to making AI accessible on a worldwide scale. By breaking down geographical and financial barriers, Google ensures that advanced AI is not just a luxury for a select few but a tool for innovation and productivity available to anyone with internet access. This widespread accessibility has the potential to drive significant change, enabling individuals and businesses around the world to harness the power of AI to enhance their capabilities, improve efficiency, and innovate in ways that were previously out of reach.

This global approach also highlights the importance of cultural and contextual relevance in AI. By making Gems available in diverse regions, Google allows users to customize these assistants to fit their specific cultural and linguistic contexts, ensuring that the AI is not just powerful but also relevant and effective. This is particularly important in areas where language and local knowledge play a crucial role in business and daily life. Through Gems, users can create AI assistants that understand and cater to their unique needs, whether that involves navigating regional market dynamics or providing services in multiple languages.

The democratization of AI through Gems can also be seen as an effort to foster innovation at all levels. By providing advanced tools to a broader audience, Google is encouraging experimentation and creativity in how AI is applied across different sectors. This could lead to new and unexpected uses for AI, driven by the ingenuity of individuals and small enterprises who now have the means to explore and implement AI-driven solutions. In this way, the availability of Gems serves as a catalyst for broader technological advancement, empowering a more diverse range of voices to contribute to the evolving AI landscape.

In essence, the democratization of AI through the rollout of Gems is about making powerful, specialized AI assistance accessible to everyone, not just those with deep pockets or technical expertise.

It's about providing the tools and opportunities for individuals and smaller entities to compete and innovate on a global stage. By extending the reach of AI and ensuring its benefits are more evenly distributed, Google is taking a significant step toward a future where advanced technology is not a privilege but a universal resource, driving progress and enhancing lives around the world.

Chapter 3: Why Gems Are a Game-Changer

The evolution of artificial intelligence has often followed a trajectory towards creating models that can handle a broad array of tasks, aiming for versatility and general applicability. This approach, while impressive in its breadth, has often resulted in AI systems that are competent in many areas but excel in none. The introduction of Gems marks a deliberate shift away from this "one-size-fits-all" philosophy, embracing the idea that specialization can unlock a level of precision and effectiveness that generalized models simply can't achieve.

General-purpose AI models, like many popular virtual assistants, are designed to perform a wide range of functions. They can help answer questions, manage schedules, play music, and provide weather updates, all with a reasonable degree of competence. However, this versatility comes at the cost of depth. When tasked with more complex, specialized queries or functions, these models often fall short, providing generic or surface-level responses that lack the nuance or detail needed for truly effective assistance. They function as helpful aides but are limited by their broad programming, which inherently lacks the capacity for deep expertise in any one area.

Gems take a different approach by focusing on task-specific excellence. Instead of trying to be all things to all people, each Gem is designed to be an expert in a particular field or function. This specialization allows them to deliver responses that are not only more relevant but also more precise, tailored to the exact needs of the user. For example, a Gem designed for coding assistance isn't just a general helper with programming; it can dive deep into specific languages, frameworks, and coding practices, offering insights and solutions that are directly applicable to the user's unique project requirements. This makes it more akin to having a skilled colleague or consultant at your disposal, rather than a jack-of-all-trades assistant.

The precision offered by Gems comes from their ability to be trained and customized for specific tasks. Users can guide their Gems to focus on the areas most relevant to them, refining the assistant's capabilities to suit their individual needs. This means that a Gem isn't just providing generic advice; it's offering tailored support that takes into account the specific context and goals of the user. In a business setting, this could mean a Gem that is finely tuned to understand market trends within a particular industry, providing data-driven insights and strategies that are far more actionable than the broad suggestions of a general-purpose AI.

This specialization is particularly valuable in fields where accuracy and detail are paramount. In healthcare, for instance, a Gem could be designed to assist with analyzing patient data, identifying patterns, and providing diagnostic support with a level of precision that general models would struggle to achieve. In education, a Gem tailored for a specific subject area can offer personalized tutoring, adapting to a student's learning style and pace to provide targeted exercises and explanations. By focusing on what they do best, Gems deliver a quality of service that significantly enhances their value and utility.

The move towards specialized AI with Gems reflects a broader understanding of how people use and benefit from artificial intelligence. In many cases, users don't need a model that can do everything; they need one that can do a specific thing exceptionally well. By honing in on particular tasks and offering deep, contextualized support, Gems address this need, providing a user experience that is both more satisfying and more effective. They transform AI from a general helper into a true partner, capable of offering expertise and insight that can make a meaningful difference in the user's work or daily life.

In this way, Gems represent a significant advancement in the field of AI, illustrating the power of specialization over generalization. They show that by focusing on doing a few things exceptionally well, AI can move beyond the limitations of broad applicability and become a more integral, impactful part of how we work, learn, and solve problems. This shift not only enhances the practical utility of AI but also opens up new possibilities for how we can leverage artificial intelligence to achieve greater precision, efficiency, and innovation in various domains.

Gems have the potential to revolutionize numerous industries by providing specialized AI assistance that adapts to the specific needs and challenges of each field. Their ability to act as personal experts, offering precise and relevant support, opens up a wide array of applications in sectors such as education, healthcare, and business, among others. By focusing on specialization, Gems can deliver insights and solutions that enhance efficiency, decision-making, and overall effectiveness in various professional environments.

In the realm of education, Gems can function as AI tutors, offering personalized learning experiences that cater to the unique needs of each student. Traditional classroom settings often struggle with the challenge of providing individualized attention to every learner, especially when dealing with large class sizes. A Gem designed for educational purposes can bridge this gap by adapting to a student's specific learning style, pace, and areas of difficulty. For instance, a student struggling with calculus can receive tailored explanations, step-by-step problem-solving guidance, and custom exercises to target their weak points. This personalized approach helps students grasp complex concepts more effectively, promoting deeper understanding and long-term retention. Additionally, educators can utilize Gems to track student progress, identify learning gaps, and suggest targeted interventions, enhancing the overall quality of education.

In healthcare, Gems can serve as diagnostic assistants, aiding medical professionals in making faster and more informed decisions. The healthcare industry generates vast amounts of data, from patient records to imaging results, and efficiently analyzing this data is crucial for accurate diagnoses and treatment plans. A Gem tailored for healthcare can process and interpret patient information, cross-referencing symptoms and medical histories with the latest research and clinical guidelines. For example, in radiology, a Gem could assist in analyzing medical images, such as X-rays or MRIs, highlighting potential areas of concern and suggesting possible diagnoses. This capability not only speeds up the diagnostic process but also reduces the likelihood of human error, contributing to better patient outcomes. While Gems are not intended to replace medical professionals, they can act as valuable support tools, enhancing the efficiency and accuracy of healthcare delivery.

In the business world, Gems can be invaluable for market analysis and understanding customer behavior. In today's fast-paced market environment, having access to timely and accurate insights is essential for staying ahead of the competition. A Gem developed for business analytics can sift through large datasets, identifying trends, patterns, and opportunities that may not be immediately apparent. For instance, it could analyze sales data, customer feedback, and market indicators to provide strategic recommendations for product development, marketing campaigns, or customer engagement strategies. By offering detailed analysis and actionable insights, these Gems enable businesses to make more informed decisions, optimize operations, and better anticipate market shifts. They can also help in segmenting customer demographics, understanding purchasing behaviors, and identifying high-value customers, all of which are crucial for targeted marketing and customer relationship management.

Beyond these examples, the applications of Gems are virtually limitless. In the legal field, they can assist with document analysis and case law research, helping lawyers prepare for cases more efficiently. In creative industries, Gems can offer support in content generation, design, and multimedia production, providing inspiration and technical assistance to artists and creators. Even in daily life, a Gem could act as a personal productivity coach, helping individuals manage tasks, set goals, and maintain focus.

The versatility and specialization of Gems make them powerful tools across a wide spectrum of uses. By offering tailored, high-level support in specific areas, they enhance the ability of individuals and organizations to operate more effectively and achieve their objectives. This move towards task-specific AI assistance marks a significant departure from the traditional, generalized AI models, illustrating how technology can be adapted to meet the diverse and nuanced demands of different fields. Through their real-world applications, Gems are poised to bring about a new era of AI integration, where intelligent assistance is not just helpful but transformative in how we learn, work, and solve complex problems.

Chapter 4: Imagen 3 – Revolutionizing AI-Generated Imagery

Imagen 3 represents a significant leap in AI-driven image generation, showcasing Google's commitment to pushing the boundaries of what's possible in the realm of visual arts and creative technology. As the latest model in Google's AI portfolio, Imagen 3 is designed to transform the way we think about digital imagery, taking simple text prompts and turning them into stunning, photorealistic visuals. This capability goes beyond mere image creation; it opens up a new world of possibilities for artists, content creators, marketers, and anyone looking to harness the power of AI in visual storytelling.

What makes Imagen 3 stand out is its remarkable ability to generate images with an unparalleled level of detail and realism. Unlike earlier models, which often produced images that felt more abstract or stylized, Imagen 3 focuses on creating visuals that blur the line between reality and imagination. It achieves this through sophisticated algorithms that understand and interpret the intricacies of texture, lighting, and composition, producing images that could easily be mistaken for photographs taken by a skilled professional. Whether it's rendering the delicate feathers of a bird in flight or capturing the intricate play of light in a sunset scene, Imagen 3 brings an extraordinary level of fidelity and nuance to AI-generated art.

One of the key advancements in Imagen 3 is its ability to process and translate natural language descriptions into highly detailed images. Users can input simple or complex text prompts—anything from "a baby dragon emerging from its egg in a magical forest" to "a bustling cityscape at dawn"—and Imagen 3 will generate visuals that accurately reflect the requested scene. This text-to-image functionality is not just about creating pretty pictures; it's about enabling a new form of creative expression where ideas and imagination can be directly translated into visual form. For artists and content creators, this tool offers a way to quickly prototype concepts, explore different visual styles, and bring abstract ideas to life without the need for extensive technical skills or resources.

Beyond its artistic capabilities, Imagen 3 also serves as a valuable tool for industries that rely heavily on high-quality visuals. In advertising, for instance, creating compelling imagery that resonates with target audiences is crucial for successful campaigns. Imagen 3 allows marketers to generate eye-catching visuals tailored to their specific messaging and audience preferences, all without the need for a professional photographer or graphic designer. This can significantly speed up the creative process, reduce costs, and allow for rapid experimentation with different visual concepts. In the realm of virtual reality, where creating immersive environments is essential, Imagen 3 can produce hyper-realistic textures and scenes that enhance the user's experience, pushing the boundaries of what's possible in VR development.

What sets Imagen 3 apart from other AI image generators is not just its technical prowess but also its focus on ethical considerations. Recognizing the potential for misuse of AI-generated imagery, Google has integrated syn ID watermarking technology into Imagen 3. This ensures that every image created by the model is subtly marked, making it easier to distinguish AI-generated content from real photographs. This measure is crucial in an era where deep fakes and misinformation are growing concerns. By incorporating such safeguards, Google demonstrates a commitment to responsible AI use, ensuring that this powerful tool is used ethically and transparently.

In summary, Imagen 3 sets a new standard for AI in visual arts by combining advanced technical capabilities with a focus on ethical use. It offers an unprecedented level of detail and realism in AI-generated images, opening up new possibilities for creative expression and practical application across various industries. Whether used for artistic exploration, marketing, or virtual reality, Imagen 3 represents a significant advancement in how we can leverage AI to create and innovate visually. By making this tool accessible and ethically grounded, Google is not just advancing the state of the art in AI image generation; it is also shaping the future of how we think about and use artificial intelligence in the creative process.

Imagen 3 stands out in the realm of AI-generated imagery by offering a seamless transformation from simple text prompts to breathtaking photorealistic visuals. This capability is more than just a technical feat; it represents a fundamental shift in how we can interact with and utilize artificial intelligence in the creative process. By allowing users to describe a scene or concept in natural language, Imagen 3 can interpret and render that description into a stunning, highly detailed image that captures the essence of the original idea. This transformation from text to art not only streamlines the creative process but also expands the horizons of what's possible in digital content creation.

One of the most remarkable aspects of Imagen 3 is its ability to capture intricate details and textures within the images it generates. Earlier AI models often struggled with producing images that felt realistic, typically resulting in outputs that were either too abstract or lacked the subtleties found in real-world visuals. Imagen 3, however, has been trained to understand and replicate the minute details that bring an image to life. This includes the complex interplay of light and shadow, the subtle gradations of color, and the nuanced textures that define different materials—whether it's the rough surface of a tree bark, the delicate feathers of a bird, or the shimmering reflection on a water surface.

For instance, if you prompt Imagen 3 with a description like "a baby dragon emerging from its egg in a magical forest," it doesn't just produce a basic image of a dragon and some trees. Instead, it dives into the specifics—rendering the dragon's scales with a lifelike sheen, capturing the delicate translucence of the egg's shell, and creating a forest backdrop with layers of depth and variety in the foliage. The resulting image is not just a visual representation of the text; it's a rich, immersive scene that conveys mood, atmosphere, and narrative in a way that feels almost tangible.

The significance of this level of detail and texture goes beyond mere aesthetics. In fields like advertising, where creating a strong visual impact is crucial, the ability to generate images that resonate with viewers on an emotional and sensory level can make all the difference. Imagen 3 allows marketers and designers to produce compelling, high-quality visuals that can be tailored to specific campaigns or audiences, all while maintaining a degree of realism and polish that would typically require extensive time and resources to achieve manually. This not only accelerates the creative process but also opens up new possibilities for visual storytelling, enabling more dynamic and engaging content.

Moreover, the advanced texture and detail capabilities of Imagen 3 are particularly valuable in applications like virtual reality and augmented reality, where the goal is to create environments that feel as real and immersive as possible. In these contexts, every element of the scene, from the texture of surfaces to the way light interacts with objects, contributes to the overall sense of presence and believability. Imagen 3 can generate the hyper-realistic textures and nuanced details needed to construct these immersive experiences, enhancing the user's sense of being transported to another world.

The ability of Imagen 3 to turn simple text into richly detailed visuals also has implications for accessibility in the creative process. Not everyone has the artistic skills or technical know-how to create high-quality images from scratch, but with Imagen 3, the barrier to entry is significantly lowered. Anyone can describe an idea or scene in words and have the AI generate a visual representation that captures their vision with remarkable fidelity. This democratization of image creation empowers a wider range of individuals to express themselves visually, whether for personal projects, educational materials, or professional content.

In summary, Imagen 3's transformation of text to art is a groundbreaking advancement that showcases the model's ability to generate images with incredible detail and texture. It elevates AI-generated imagery to a new level of realism and artistry, providing tools that are not only functional but also capable of producing visually stunning results. By focusing on the subtleties that make an image feel real and evocative, Imagen 3 offers a powerful resource for artists, designers, marketers, and anyone looking to bring their ideas to life in vivid, photorealistic detail. This capability is reshaping the landscape of digital art and content creation, making high-quality visual storytelling more accessible and versatile than ever before.

Chapter 5: Applications of Imagen 3

Imagen 3's capabilities extend far beyond simply generating beautiful images. Its role in various industries showcases how advanced AI-driven image generation can revolutionize the way businesses and creators approach visual content. By producing highly detailed and photorealistic images from text prompts, Imagen 3 serves as a powerful tool in sectors like advertising and virtual reality, where the quality and impact of visuals are paramount.

In the world of advertising, the ability to create compelling imagery quickly and effectively is a critical component of successful marketing campaigns. Traditional methods of producing high-quality visuals often involve lengthy processes, including concept development, photography, graphic design, and post-production. These steps not only require significant time and resources but also demand specialized skills and equipment. Imagen 3 simplifies this process by allowing marketers to generate stunning visuals with just a text prompt, eliminating many of the logistical and creative bottlenecks associated with traditional content creation.

For instance, a company looking to launch a new product can use Imagen 3 to create a series of eye-catching promotional images that highlight the product's features in various settings. Whether it's a sleek new gadget showcased in a futuristic environment or a lifestyle product set against a backdrop of everyday scenarios, Imagen 3 can generate visuals that are tailored to the campaign's narrative and target audience. This level of customization and efficiency enables marketers to experiment with different visual concepts, iterate quickly, and adapt to changing trends or market feedback without the need for costly photo shoots or extensive graphic design work.

Moreover, the photorealistic quality of Imagen 3's outputs ensures that the visuals not only capture attention but also convey a sense of authenticity and professionalism. In advertising, where first impressions are crucial, having high-quality, believable imagery can make a significant difference in how a brand or product is perceived. Imagen 3 provides the means to produce such imagery consistently and at scale, helping businesses create more engaging and effective marketing materials that resonate with consumers.

In the realm of virtual reality (VR), the importance of visual fidelity cannot be overstated. The success of a VR experience hinges on its ability to immerse users in a believable and captivating environment. Every element within this virtual space, from the textures on walls to the way light filters through a window, contributes to the overall sense of presence and realism. Imagen 3 excels in generating the kind of hyper-realistic textures and details needed to enhance these virtual worlds, making them more convincing and engaging.

For VR developers, Imagen 3 offers a valuable resource for creating detailed assets that can populate and enrich their environments. Whether it's crafting the weathered look of an ancient stone temple or the intricate pattern on a futuristic control panel, Imagen 3 can produce high-quality textures that add depth and nuance to virtual settings. This capability not only elevates the visual quality of VR experiences but also streamlines the asset creation process, allowing developers to focus more on the design and interaction aspects of their projects.

Beyond enhancing the visual elements of virtual reality, Imagen 3's ability to generate specific and detailed images can also aid in the development of augmented reality (AR) applications. In AR, where digital elements are overlaid onto the real world, the seamless integration of these elements relies on their visual realism and coherence with the surrounding environment. Imagen 3 can be used to create AR assets that blend naturally with the physical world, making interactions more intuitive and immersive for users.

The applications of Imagen 3 in advertising and virtual reality are just the beginning. Its potential extends to any field where high-quality visuals play a crucial role, including e-commerce, where product imagery can influence purchasing decisions, or architecture and real estate, where detailed renderings of spaces can aid in planning and marketing. By offering an accessible way to generate complex and realistic visuals, Imagen 3 not only changes how images are created but also how they are utilized across various industries.

In summary, Imagen 3 transcends the realm of creating "pretty pictures" by serving as a versatile tool that meets the demands of industries where visual impact is key. In advertising, it provides a means to produce customized, high-quality visuals that enhance campaign effectiveness. In virtual reality, it offers the capability to generate textures and details that make immersive environments more believable and engaging. These applications demonstrate the transformative potential of Imagen 3, showcasing how advanced AI can be harnessed to revolutionize visual content creation and utilization in diverse sectors.

In the age of rapidly advancing artificial intelligence, ethical considerations have become a critical part of the conversation, particularly when it comes to AI-generated content. Recognizing the potential implications of creating images that closely mimic reality, Google has taken a proactive stance with Imagen 3 by incorporating syn ID watermarking technology. This built-in safeguard ensures that every image produced by Imagen 3 contains a subtle, identifiable marker, helping to distinguish AI-generated content from real photographs. By doing so, Google addresses a range of ethical concerns, including the proliferation of deep fakes and the spread of misinformation, both of which pose significant challenges in today's digital landscape.

Syn ID watermarking serves as a digital signature embedded within each image generated by Imagen 3. While invisible to the naked eye, this watermark can be detected and verified, providing a means to trace the origin of the image. This technology is crucial in an era where AI-generated content is becoming increasingly sophisticated and difficult to differentiate from actual photographs. The risk here lies in the potential misuse of such realistic imagery, where AI-created visuals could be passed off as genuine, leading to scenarios where trust in digital media is undermined. By ensuring that Imagen 3's outputs are marked, Google provides a layer of transparency and accountability, helping users and platforms identify AI-generated content and prevent its misuse.

The importance of distinguishing AI-generated content from real photographs extends beyond preventing deception. In a world where images are a primary mode of communication and information dissemination, the line between reality and fabrication can have profound implications. For instance, manipulated or fabricated images can be used to distort facts, manipulate public opinion, or propagate false narratives. These concerns are particularly acute in the context of deep fakes, where AI-generated imagery can be used to create convincing but entirely fictitious representations of people, events, or situations. By clearly marking AI-generated images, Google is taking steps to mitigate the risk of such technologies being used to deceive or mislead.

Moreover, the incorporation of syn ID watermarking aligns with broader efforts to establish ethical guidelines and best practices for AI development and deployment. As AI continues to evolve and permeate various aspects of society, establishing norms around transparency, authenticity, and responsible use becomes increasingly important. By embedding a means of identifying AI-generated content within Imagen 3, Google sets a precedent for how advanced image generation tools can be developed with ethical considerations at the forefront. This approach not only protects the integrity of digital content but also fosters trust in AI technologies by showing a commitment to responsible innovation.

Addressing concerns around deep fakes and misinformation is a crucial aspect of this ethical approach. Deep fakes, which involve the use of AI to create highly realistic but entirely fabricated images or videos, have raised alarm due to their potential to cause harm in various contexts, from personal defamation to political manipulation. The ability to generate convincing fake content has serious implications for privacy, security, and the trustworthiness of media. By embedding identifiers in AI-generated images, Google provides a tool for verifying the authenticity of visual content, making it more difficult for deep fakes to go undetected and be used maliciously.

In addition to combating the spread of misinformation, this technology also plays a role in ensuring that the creative use of AI remains ethical and respectful. As AI-generated imagery becomes more prevalent in art, advertising, and media, there is a need to acknowledge and attribute the role of AI in the creative process. Syn ID watermarking helps maintain this transparency, ensuring that audiences are aware when a piece of content has been produced with the assistance of AI. This awareness fosters an environment where AI is seen not as a tool for deception, but as an enabler of new forms of creativity and expression, used responsibly and with integrity.

In conclusion, Google's incorporation of syn ID watermarking technology in Imagen 3 reflects a thoughtful and forward-looking approach to the ethical challenges posed by AI-generated content. By marking each image produced by the model, Google addresses the need for transparency and accountability, helping to distinguish AI-created visuals from real photographs. This measure is crucial in preventing the misuse of AI-generated imagery, particularly in the context of deep fakes and misinformation. It represents a commitment to developing AI in a manner that prioritizes ethical considerations, fostering trust and responsibility in the ongoing evolution of artificial intelligence.

Chapter 6: Google's Position in the AI Market

The AI market is currently a dynamic and highly competitive landscape, with major tech companies racing to push the boundaries of what artificial intelligence can achieve. Each player in this field—whether it's OpenAI, Microsoft, Meta (formerly Facebook), or Google—brings its unique strengths and strategies to the table, driving innovation and setting new standards for AI capabilities. These companies are not just developing AI models; they are creating ecosystems of tools and platforms designed to integrate seamlessly into various aspects of technology and everyday life.

OpenAI has been a prominent name in the field, known for its development of advanced language models like GPT-3 and GPT-4. These models have demonstrated impressive capabilities in natural language understanding and generation, finding applications in everything from customer service chatbots to creative writing and coding assistance. OpenAI's focus has been on creating versatile, general-purpose AI that can handle a broad range of tasks. This versatility has made its models highly popular and widely adopted, serving as the backbone for many AI-driven applications across different industries.

Microsoft has also made significant strides in AI, particularly through its Azure cloud platform and the integration of AI into its suite of productivity tools. With services like Azure Cognitive Services and AI-powered features in Microsoft Office, the company has focused on embedding AI into the fabric of business operations, enhancing productivity, and providing intelligent solutions for data analysis, automation, and decision-making. Microsoft's approach often emphasizes seamless integration and accessibility, enabling businesses of all sizes to harness the power of AI without requiring extensive technical expertise.

Meta, on the other hand, has been exploring AI through the lens of social interaction and virtual experiences. With initiatives like AI-driven content moderation on platforms like Facebook and Instagram, as well as developments in virtual and augmented reality, Meta is leveraging AI to enhance user engagement and create more immersive digital environments. The company's investment in AI research aims to understand and predict human behavior, improving the ways people connect and interact in the digital world.

In this competitive arena, Google's approach with Gems and Imagen 3 sets it apart by emphasizing specialization, personalization, and ethical considerations. While many competitors have focused on building broad, general-purpose models, Google has taken a different route by developing AI tools that excel in specific tasks and cater to individual user needs. This focus on specialization is evident in the design of Gems, which are highly tailored assistants capable of performing specific functions exceptionally well. By providing users with the ability to create personal experts, Google offers a level of customization and depth that general-purpose models do not typically provide.

The differentiation continues with Imagen 3, where Google has concentrated on advancing the capabilities of AI-generated imagery. Unlike general AI models that may include image generation as one of many features, Imagen 3 is dedicated to transforming text prompts into highly detailed and photorealistic visuals. This focus allows Google to set a new standard in the visual arts, providing tools that not only produce stunning imagery but also incorporate ethical safeguards like syn ID watermarking technology. By ensuring that AI-generated images are clearly identifiable, Google addresses concerns around deep fakes and misinformation, adding a layer of trust and accountability to its offerings.

Furthermore, Google's strategic emphasis on democratizing AI is another distinguishing factor.

By making Gems accessible to a wide audience, including small businesses, freelancers, and individuals, Google is not just targeting large enterprises with its advanced tools. This inclusivity contrasts with some competitors' models, which may require significant resources or technical expertise to implement effectively. Google's approach aims to level the playing field, empowering users from diverse backgrounds to harness the power of AI in meaningful ways.

Another aspect of Google's differentiation lies in its commitment to ethical AI development. While other companies are certainly aware of the ethical challenges posed by AI, Google's integration of ethical considerations into the core functionality of its products, like the watermarking in Imagen 3, demonstrates a proactive stance on these issues. This approach aligns with growing concerns about the potential misuse of AI, ensuring that as the technology advances, it does so in a manner that prioritizes transparency, authenticity, and responsible use.

In summary, while the AI market is crowded with innovative players, Google's approach with Gems and Imagen 3 stands out for its focus on specialization, personalization, and ethical considerations. By developing task-specific assistants and advanced image generation tools, Google offers a unique proposition that differs from the general-purpose models of competitors like OpenAI, Microsoft, and Meta. This strategy not only enhances the practical utility of AI but also addresses some of the key ethical challenges associated with its use, positioning Google as a leader in the responsible and transformative deployment of artificial intelligence.

In the rapidly evolving field of artificial intelligence, the move towards specialization marks a significant shift from the earlier focus on creating broad, general-purpose models. This change is driven by a recognition that while versatile AI systems have their place, there is immense value in developing tools that excel in specific domains. Google's introduction of Gems and Imagen 3 exemplifies this shift, offering highly specialized AI assistants and image generation capabilities that cater to distinct user needs. This focus on specialization is coupled with a strong emphasis on ethical considerations, highlighting the importance of developing AI that not only performs well but also aligns with responsible use and transparency.

Specialization in AI means developing systems that are designed to handle particular tasks with a high degree of expertise. Instead of attempting to create a single model that can do everything reasonably well, the goal is to create AI tools that can perform specific functions exceptionally. Gems are a prime example of this approach. Unlike general-purpose AI models that offer a wide range of capabilities, Gems are designed to provide in-depth assistance tailored to individual tasks, whether it's coding, marketing strategy, or personalized tutoring. By honing in on a particular area, Gems can offer more precise, relevant, and actionable support, acting as digital experts that enhance productivity and decision-making.

This specialization is particularly valuable in complex fields where a deep understanding of the subject matter is crucial. In healthcare, for instance, a general AI might provide basic diagnostic support, but a specialized Gem can delve into patient data, identify patterns, and offer insights that are directly applicable to clinical decision-making. Similarly, in education, a Gem tailored for advanced mathematics can adapt to a student's learning style, providing custom exercises and explanations that facilitate a deeper comprehension of challenging concepts. By creating tools that are experts in their fields, Google is redefining the role of AI, moving from a general helper to a true partner in various professional and personal endeavors.

Alongside this push for specialization, Google places a strong emphasis on ethical considerations in AI development. As AI becomes increasingly integrated into daily life and decision-making processes, the ethical implications of its use cannot be overlooked. The power of AI to generate realistic images, analyze vast amounts of data, or influence user behavior carries with it the potential for misuse, whether intentional or accidental. Recognizing this, Google has taken steps to ensure that its AI tools, like Imagen 3, are developed and deployed with a focus on transparency, accountability, and user trust.

A key component of this ethical approach is the incorporation of syn ID watermarking technology into Imagen 3. This technology embeds a subtle, detectable marker within every image generated by the model, making it possible to identify and distinguish AI-generated content from real photographs. In an era where deep fakes and manipulated imagery pose serious threats to trust and authenticity in digital media, this measure is a critical safeguard. It not only helps prevent the misuse of AI-generated images but also supports the broader effort to maintain the integrity of visual information. By ensuring that AI-generated content can be traced and verified, Google is taking a proactive stance on combating misinformation and ensuring that its technology is used responsibly.

Moreover, Google's emphasis on ethical use extends beyond technical safeguards to encompass the broader implications of AI in society. The company recognizes that as AI tools become more powerful and widespread, questions around privacy, data security, and the potential impact on jobs and decision-making become increasingly important. By embedding ethical considerations into the design and functionality of its AI products, Google aims to foster a culture of responsible innovation. This includes not only preventing harmful applications of AI but also ensuring that its tools are used to enhance human capabilities and contribute positively to society.

In practice, this means that while Gems and Imagen 3 are designed to be powerful and versatile, they are also built with mechanisms to ensure their use aligns with ethical standards. For instance, the transparency provided by syn ID watermarking in Imagen 3 helps maintain public trust in digital content by making the AI origin of images clear. Similarly, the tailored, specialized nature of Gems supports ethical use by ensuring that the AI's guidance is relevant and accurate, reducing the risk of incorrect or misleading outputs in sensitive areas like healthcare or education.

In summary, Google's focus on creating highly specialized AI tools and emphasizing ethical considerations in their development represents a thoughtful and responsible approach to artificial intelligence. By prioritizing specialization, Google provides users with AI that is not just broadly capable but expertly designed for specific tasks, enhancing effectiveness and user experience. At the same time, the incorporation of ethical safeguards like syn ID watermarking ensures that these advanced tools are used in a manner that is transparent, accountable, and aligned with the broader societal need for trustworthy and responsible AI. This dual focus on specialization and ethical use sets a standard for how AI can be developed and deployed in a way that is both innovative and conscientious.

Chapter 7: The Implications of Gemini's Upgrades

Artificial intelligence, once a concept confined to science fiction and specialized industries, is now weaving itself into the fabric of everyday life. Tools like Google's Gems and Imagen 3 exemplify this integration, bringing advanced AI capabilities directly into the routines of individuals and businesses alike. From enhancing productivity to fostering creativity, these tools are becoming essential in various aspects of daily activities, influencing how we work, learn, communicate, and create.

In the realm of daily routines, Gems serve as personalized assistants, offering specialized support tailored to individual needs. Imagine a professional who uses a Gem to streamline their workflow—automating tasks like email sorting, managing schedules, or even providing real-time market analysis for business decisions. This level of assistance not only saves time but also enhances decision-making by offering insights that are specific and actionable. For students, Gems can act as personal tutors, adapting to their learning styles and providing targeted exercises that help them grasp complex subjects more effectively. By serving as dedicated experts in their respective fields, Gems bring a level of support that transforms how people approach their daily challenges, making AI an integral part of personal and professional growth.

In creative pursuits, Imagen 3 is revolutionizing the way visual content is produced and consumed. For artists, designers, and marketers, the ability to generate high-quality, photorealistic images from simple text prompts opens up new avenues for creativity and experimentation. It eliminates many of the barriers that traditionally accompany visual content creation, such as the need for advanced graphic design skills or expensive photo shoots. Now, anyone with an idea can bring it to life visually, whether it's for a marketing campaign, a virtual reality environment, or personal artistic expression. This democratization of creative tools means that AI is not just a passive part of our routines but an active participant in helping us realize our ideas and aspirations.

The integration of AI into everyday life offers numerous benefits. It enhances efficiency, enabling people to accomplish tasks more quickly and with greater precision. In the workplace, this can translate to improved productivity, as repetitive or time-consuming tasks are delegated to AI assistants, freeing up human resources for more strategic or creative endeavors. In personal life, AI can help manage daily responsibilities, from organizing household tasks to offering personalized fitness or wellness guidance. This kind of support can lead to a better work-life balance, as individuals have more time and energy to devote to what matters most to them.

Additionally, the widespread adoption of AI tools like Gems and Imagen 3 has the potential to foster innovation across various sectors. By making advanced capabilities accessible to a broader audience, AI can serve as a catalyst for new ideas and solutions. Small businesses and freelancers, for example, can leverage AI to compete with larger enterprises by gaining insights and efficiencies that were previously out of reach. In education, AI-driven personalized learning can help bridge gaps and provide equal opportunities for students with diverse needs and backgrounds. In healthcare, AI can support faster and more accurate diagnoses, improving patient outcomes and potentially saving lives.

However, the growing presence of AI in daily life also brings challenges that need to be addressed. One of the primary concerns is data privacy. As AI systems become more integrated into our routines, they often require access to personal data to function effectively. This raises questions about how that data is used, stored, and protected. Users need to be assured that their information is handled with care and that there are safeguards in place to prevent misuse or unauthorized access. Companies like Google are aware of these concerns and are working to implement robust data security measures, but the issue of privacy remains a central consideration in the widespread adoption of AI.

Another challenge is the potential impact on employment. As AI takes on more roles and tasks traditionally performed by humans, there is concern about job displacement. While AI can enhance productivity and open up new opportunities, it may also render certain jobs obsolete, particularly those involving repetitive or routine tasks. This shift necessitates a broader conversation about how to prepare the workforce for an economy increasingly driven by automation and AI. It involves investing in education and training programs that help people develop skills suited to the evolving job market, focusing on areas where human ingenuity, creativity, and interpersonal skills remain essential.

Moreover, the reliance on AI tools raises questions about the potential for over-dependence. As we integrate AI more deeply into our daily lives, there's a risk that we might rely too heavily on these tools, potentially diminishing our own problem-solving abilities or critical thinking skills. Finding the right balance between leveraging AI's capabilities and maintaining our human touch and judgment is crucial.

In conclusion, the impact of AI tools like Gems and Imagen 3 on everyday life is profound, offering significant benefits in terms of efficiency, creativity, and innovation. They are transforming how we approach tasks, solve problems, and express ourselves, making advanced technology an integral part of our routines. However, this integration also brings challenges, particularly around data privacy, job displacement, and the potential for over-reliance on AI. Addressing these challenges requires a thoughtful and responsible approach to AI adoption, ensuring that as we embrace the benefits of these powerful tools, we also navigate the ethical and societal implications with care.

As artificial intelligence becomes increasingly integrated into daily life, concerns around data privacy and job displacement have come to the forefront of discussions about its impact. The adoption of AI tools like Google's Gems and Imagen 3 brings with it a wealth of opportunities, but also raises important questions about how personal data is managed and the potential implications for the workforce. Addressing these concerns is crucial to ensure that AI is used responsibly and that its benefits are realized in a way that respects individual privacy and supports the evolving job market.

Data privacy is a significant concern as AI systems often rely on access to large amounts of personal information to function effectively. Whether it's a Gem assisting with personalized learning, healthcare diagnostics, or market analysis, these tools need to collect and process data to provide tailored and relevant responses. This data can include sensitive information such as health records, financial details, or personal preferences, raising questions about how this information is stored, used, and protected. Users are rightfully cautious about the potential for misuse, unauthorized access, or breaches that could compromise their privacy.

To address these concerns, companies like Google are implementing robust data security measures, ensuring that user data is handled with the utmost care and confidentiality. Encryption, anonymization, and secure storage practices are essential components of this approach, minimizing the risk of data breaches and unauthorized access. Furthermore, transparency is key; users should be informed about what data is being collected, how it is used, and the measures in place to protect it. Providing users with control over their data, including options to manage permissions or delete information, helps build trust and ensures that AI systems are used ethically and responsibly.

Beyond technical safeguards, there is also the issue of data ownership and consent. It's important that users have the autonomy to decide what data they are willing to share and for what purposes. This involves clear communication and consent mechanisms, allowing individuals to make informed decisions about their data. By prioritizing user rights and privacy, AI developers can create systems that not only provide value but also respect individual autonomy and promote ethical use.

Job displacement is another significant concern associated with the rise of AI. As AI systems become more capable of performing tasks that were traditionally carried out by humans, there is a legitimate fear that automation could lead to job losses, particularly in roles that involve routine or repetitive tasks. For example, AI-driven customer service bots can handle a large volume of inquiries without the need for human intervention, and

AI-powered diagnostic tools can assist in healthcare analysis, potentially reducing the demand for certain roles in these fields.

However, while AI may replace some jobs, it also has the potential to create new opportunities and transform the nature of work. The key is to view AI as a tool that augments human capabilities rather than one that simply replaces them. In many cases, AI can take over mundane or time-consuming tasks, freeing up individuals to focus on more complex, creative, and strategic aspects of their work. For example, in a business setting, a Gem can automate data analysis and reporting, allowing employees to concentrate on interpreting the results, developing strategies, and making informed decisions. In healthcare, AI can handle the initial data processing, enabling medical professionals to spend more time on patient care and complex diagnostics.

To navigate the potential impact on employment, there is a need for proactive measures that support workers in adapting to an AI-driven economy. This includes investing in education and retraining programs that equip individuals with the skills needed to thrive in a changing job market. Emphasizing areas where human skills are irreplaceable, such as creativity, emotional intelligence, and complex problem-solving, can help ensure that the workforce is prepared for the new opportunities that AI presents. Additionally, fostering a culture of lifelong learning and adaptability is crucial, as it enables workers to stay relevant and agile in the face of technological advancements.

Moreover, the integration of AI into various industries can lead to the creation of entirely new roles and sectors. As businesses and organizations adopt AI, there is a growing need for professionals who can develop, implement, and manage these systems. This includes roles in AI ethics, data analysis, AI-human interaction design, and more. The development and maintenance of AI technologies require human input, creativity, and oversight, creating opportunities for skilled workers to contribute to this evolving field.

In conclusion, the increasing integration of AI into our lives brings with it important considerations around data privacy and job displacement. Ensuring that user data is handled securely and ethically is paramount, requiring transparency, user control, and robust security measures. At the same time, while AI has the potential to disrupt traditional job roles, it also offers opportunities to transform the nature of work and create new professions. By approaching these challenges with a focus on ethical use, education, and adaptability, we can harness the benefits of AI while mitigating its risks, paving the way for a future where AI enhances rather than diminishes human potential.

Chapter 8: The Future of Google's Gemini and AI

As Google continues to innovate and expand its Gemini platform, the future holds exciting possibilities for further advancements and enhancements. Given the rapid pace of AI development and the increasing integration of these technologies into everyday life, it's reasonable to anticipate that future updates to Gemini will build upon its current capabilities, introducing new features and refinements that push the boundaries of what AI can achieve.

One potential direction for the future of Gemini is the development of even more specialized Gems tailored for niche industries. Currently, Gems are already designed to provide task-specific assistance in areas such as coding, marketing, and personalized learning. However, the scope for specialization is vast, and there is an opportunity to create Gems that cater to highly specific sectors or roles. For example, in the legal industry, we could see the emergence of Gems designed to assist with complex tasks like legal research, contract analysis, and case preparation, providing lawyers with an AI partner that can quickly sift through vast amounts of legal documents and precedents to find relevant information.

Similarly, in fields like scientific research, Gems could be developed to assist with data analysis, hypothesis generation, and even experimental design. Such Gems would be equipped to handle the unique demands of scientific inquiry, helping researchers navigate the complexities of their data, identify patterns, and suggest potential avenues for further investigation. This level of specialization could accelerate the pace of discovery and innovation across various scientific disciplines, offering tools that enhance the capabilities of researchers and facilitate more efficient workflows.

Another area where we might see more specialized Gems is in creative industries such as music production, filmmaking, and digital art. For instance, a Gem tailored for music producers could assist in composing, arranging, and mixing tracks, offering suggestions based on genre, mood, and style preferences. In filmmaking, a specialized Gem could aid in script analysis, scene planning, and even editing, providing filmmakers with a virtual assistant that enhances the creative process. By focusing on the unique needs and workflows of these industries, specialized Gems can become invaluable tools that support and amplify human creativity.

In addition to creating more specialized Gems, future updates to the Gemini platform might also focus on enhancing the adaptability and learning capabilities of these AI assistants. As users interact with their Gems, the AI could become more attuned to individual preferences, styles, and requirements, offering increasingly personalized and context-aware support. This could involve the integration of more advanced machine learning techniques that allow Gems to continually learn and improve based on user feedback and interactions. The result would be AI assistants that not only specialize in certain tasks but also evolve over time to become more effective and aligned with the user's evolving needs.

Moreover, we can expect future developments to incorporate greater interoperability between Gems and other AI tools or platforms. This integration could enable users to seamlessly connect their Gems with other digital systems, such as customer relationship management (CRM) software, project management tools, or data analytics platforms. By creating a more interconnected AI ecosystem, Google could enhance the overall utility of Gems, making them an even more integral part of various workflows and applications.

Given Google's emphasis on ethical considerations, it is also likely that future updates to Gemini will continue to focus on responsible AI use. This could involve implementing new safeguards and transparency measures, particularly as AI becomes more sophisticated and its potential applications broaden. For instance, enhancements to syn ID watermarking in Imagen 3 or similar mechanisms could be introduced to address emerging challenges in distinguishing AI-generated content from real-world media. Additionally, Google may develop new features that provide users with greater control over how their data is used and how their Gems operate, ensuring that privacy and ethical use remain at the forefront of AI development.

Looking ahead, there is also the possibility that Gemini will explore more collaborative AI experiences, where multiple Gems can work together to tackle complex, multi-faceted problems. This collaborative approach could involve different Gems specializing in various aspects of a project, such as one Gem focusing on data analysis while another handles project management and coordination. By enabling Gems to communicate and collaborate, the platform could offer a more holistic solution to complex challenges, leveraging the strengths of multiple AI assistants to achieve better outcomes.

The future of Google's Gemini platform holds immense potential for further innovation and specialization. We can anticipate the development of more specialized Gems tailored to niche industries, enhanced adaptability and learning capabilities, greater integration with other digital tools, and a continued focus on ethical use. As AI technology continues to evolve, Gemini is poised to become an even more powerful and versatile platform, offering tools that not only transform how we work and create but also align with the values of transparency, privacy, and responsible use. The journey of Gemini is just beginning, and the possibilities for its future are as diverse and exciting as the fields it aims to revolutionize.

The landscape of artificial intelligence is continuously evolving, driven by rapid advancements in technology and an expanding understanding of AI's potential applications. As AI becomes increasingly sophisticated, its role in society is set to grow even further, influencing not just how we interact with technology but also how we address complex challenges in various sectors such as healthcare, education, and environmental sustainability. This ongoing evolution brings with it both opportunities for unprecedented innovation and the need for a careful balance between progress and ethical responsibility.

One of the key trends in the evolution of AI is the move towards greater specialization and contextual understanding. While current AI models like Google's Gems and Imagen 3 offer a high degree of task-specific expertise, the future will likely see even more refined and context-aware AI systems. These systems will not only perform specialized tasks with precision but also understand the nuances of their environment and user preferences. For instance, future AI could provide more empathetic and contextually appropriate interactions in healthcare, understanding patient emotions and adjusting its responses accordingly to provide comfort and support alongside technical assistance.

Furthermore, the integration of AI into the fabric of everyday life is expected to deepen. As AI becomes more embedded in consumer devices, household appliances, and personal assistants, it will play an increasingly central role in managing day-to-day activities. Imagine a future where your home's AI system not only manages energy consumption based on your habits but also anticipates your needs, adjusting the environment for optimal comfort and convenience. In the workplace, AI will continue to evolve from being a tool that assists with tasks to becoming a collaborative partner that can help strategize, innovate, and drive decision-making processes.

Another anticipated development is the convergence of AI with other emerging technologies like quantum computing and blockchain. Quantum computing has the potential to vastly accelerate AI processing capabilities, allowing for more complex models and faster data analysis. This could lead to breakthroughs in areas such as drug discovery, climate modeling, and financial forecasting, where the computational demands are extraordinarily high. Blockchain technology, on the other hand, could play a role in enhancing the security and transparency of AI systems, ensuring that data used in AI models is handled ethically and securely, and providing a verifiable record of AI decision-making processes.

Despite these exciting prospects, the ongoing evolution of AI also demands a heightened focus on responsibility and ethics. As AI systems become more autonomous and capable of making decisions that impact human lives, the need to ensure these systems operate in a manner that is fair, transparent, and aligned with societal values becomes paramount. This balance between innovation and responsibility is crucial for building public trust in AI technologies and ensuring their positive impact on society.

One aspect of this balance is addressing issues related to data privacy and consent. As AI systems increasingly rely on personal data to provide tailored services, it is essential to establish clear guidelines on how this data is collected, used, and protected. Users should have control over their information and be able to make informed decisions about their privacy. Future AI developments will need to incorporate robust privacy-preserving techniques, such as federated learning and differential privacy, which allow AI to learn from data without compromising individual privacy.

Another ethical consideration is the potential for bias in AI systems. As AI models are trained on vast datasets, there is a risk that they may inadvertently learn and replicate biases present in the data, leading to unfair or discriminatory outcomes. The future of AI development will require a concerted effort to identify, mitigate, and eliminate such biases, ensuring that AI operates equitably and inclusively. This involves not only refining algorithms but also critically examining the datasets used to train these models and striving for diversity and representation in AI research and development teams.

Moreover, the increasing autonomy of AI systems raises questions about accountability and governance. As AI takes on more decision-making roles, it becomes important to establish clear frameworks for responsibility. Who is accountable when an AI system makes a mistake or when its actions have unintended consequences? These are questions that need to be addressed as we develop and deploy more advanced AI systems. Establishing regulatory frameworks and industry standards will be vital in guiding the ethical use of AI, ensuring that innovation does not come at the expense of safety, fairness, or societal well-being.

There is also the broader societal impact to consider, particularly in relation to employment and the future of work. As AI continues to automate tasks and streamline processes, there will be a shift in the job market, with some roles becoming obsolete while new ones emerge. Preparing the workforce for this transition through education, reskilling, and the promotion of AI literacy is essential to ensure that the benefits of AI are shared equitably and that individuals are equipped to adapt to a changing economic landscape.

In summary, the ongoing evolution of AI is poised to bring transformative changes to various aspects of life, offering the potential for significant advancements in efficiency, creativity, and problem-solving. However, this evolution must be guided by a careful balance between innovation and ethical responsibility. As we navigate the complexities of integrating AI more deeply into society, it is crucial to address challenges related to privacy, bias, accountability, and the future of work.

By prioritizing responsible development and deployment, we can ensure that the advancements in AI contribute to a future that is not only technologically advanced but also just, inclusive, and aligned with the values that underpin a healthy, functioning society.

Conclusion

The AI revolution is just beginning, and as we stand on the cusp of a new era in technological advancement, the possibilities seem boundless. Artificial intelligence has already demonstrated its transformative potential, reshaping industries, enhancing everyday life, and opening up new avenues for creativity and innovation. From the personalized expertise of Gems to the stunning visual capabilities of Imagen 3, AI is not merely a tool for automation; it is a catalyst for change, pushing the boundaries of what we can achieve. Yet, as we look toward the future, it's clear that we are only scratching the surface of AI's capabilities.

In the years to come, AI is poised to become even more integral to our lives. It will continue to evolve, becoming more sophisticated, contextually aware, and seamlessly integrated into the world around us. The advancements in specialized AI, personalized assistance, and ethical safeguards that we see today are just the beginning. As AI learns to understand and adapt to human needs more deeply, it will unlock new possibilities for enhancing productivity, creativity, and problem-solving across a myriad of fields. The impact of this revolution will be felt in every corner of society, from healthcare and education to business and the arts.

However, with this incredible potential comes a responsibility to engage with AI developments thoughtfully and ethically. As AI becomes more powerful and autonomous, the importance of guiding its evolution with a strong ethical framework cannot be overstated. This is not just a task for developers and technologists but for all of us as a society. It involves critically examining how we use AI, the data it relies on, and the decisions it makes. It requires us to ask tough questions about privacy, accountability, and fairness, ensuring that the technologies we build serve the common good and respect individual rights.

Staying informed and engaged with the ongoing developments in AI is crucial. As these technologies become more embedded in our daily lives, understanding how they work and their potential impact empowers us to make informed decisions and contribute to shaping their future. By actively participating in discussions about AI, advocating for ethical use, and supporting responsible innovation, we can help steer the course of this revolution in a direction that benefits everyone. This engagement is key to ensuring that AI not only advances our capabilities but also aligns with our values and aspirations.

Final thoughts on the future of AI highlight the delicate balance between embracing change and being mindful of its broader implications. The rapid pace of AI development offers immense opportunities for growth and improvement in virtually every sector. Yet, it also challenges us to navigate new ethical, social, and economic landscapes. As we harness the power of AI, we must remain vigilant in addressing issues of data privacy, bias, and the potential for job displacement. By prioritizing ethical considerations and implementing safeguards, we can work towards a future where AI is a force for positive change, enhancing human potential while preserving our core values.

Embracing the AI revolution means recognizing its transformative power while also committing to responsible stewardship. It is about leveraging AI's capabilities to solve complex problems, improve lives, and drive progress, all while ensuring that we remain in control of the technology we create. By fostering an environment of transparency, accountability, and inclusivity, we can ensure that the advancements in AI lead to a future that is not only technologically advanced but also just, equitable, and reflective of the diverse society we live in.

In conclusion, the journey of AI is only just beginning, and its impact on the world is poised to grow exponentially in the coming years. As we witness this unfolding revolution, it is imperative that we stay informed, engaged, and ethically grounded. By doing so, we can help shape a future where AI serves as a powerful ally in enhancing our lives and addressing some of the most pressing challenges we face. This is a pivotal moment, and how we choose to navigate it will determine the role that AI plays in our society for generations to come.